Dais

poems by

Francis Klein

Finishing Line Press
Georgetown, Kentucky

Dais

*For Wilma Lodova
and Jan Loewy*

Copyright © 2017 by Francis Klein
ISBN 978-1-63534-092-1 First Edition
All rights reserved under International and Pan-American Copyright Conventions. No part of this book may be reproduced in any manner whatsoever without written permission from the publisher, except in the case of brief quotations embodied in critical articles and reviews.

ACKNOWLEDGMENTS

Obituary information based on articles in *The New York Times*.

"Herschel Schacter" has been published in *Mudfish 18*.

Publisher: Leah Maines

Editor: Christen Kincaid

Cover Art: Susan Weintraub

Author Photo: Amy Bolger

Cover Design: Elizabeth Maines

Printed in the USA on acid-free paper.
Order online: www.finishinglinepress.com
also available on amazon.com

Author inquiries and mail orders:
Finishing Line Press
P. O. Box 1626
Georgetown, Kentucky 40324
U. S. A.

Table of Contents

Parsha
Shemini 1
Vayikra 2
Behar-Bechukotai 3
Shoftim 4
Ki Tetze 5
Ki Tavo 6
Genesis 7

Argentine Tangos
Freestyles 8
Slow Waltz 10
Ballroom Tango 11
Hustle 12
Fandango 13
Continuous Salida 14
Diana 15
Regatta 16
Starfish 17
Queen 18

Ferncliffe
Paul Soldner 19
Ardis James 20
Frank W. Lewis 21
Herschel Schacter 22
Alice Kober 23
Charles Rosen 24

Dais
Track 25
Jacob 26
Crossing 27
Siesta 28
Liberty 29
Hammerhead 30
Hydrangeas 31

Shemini

On the eighth day,
I left the temple.
I hung my tux
back up in the closet,
packed in cedar chips.

The scent of sandalwood
in the sleeping mind
brought me to you,
myrrh, sweat,
amber loops.

Books were the goats
I sacrificed
on the altar of the future,
my bindings broken, wounds,
the stitches loose.

Take me with you
into the sky's absolute blue,
the songs sung
on the Temple Mount,
the oil of the eternal.

I am yours
to find
in these vestments,
the needle's eye
in the pockets of the stones.

Vayikra

I came later,
the first of the last born,
weak in the wrists.

I swung under the turnstile
once, caught in a dare,
the token victim,
sacrificial lamb
for the older kids.

The train that will come
has already stopped
at this station.
The tracks are fixed.

And the child riding
in that distant system,
sitting on the CC's scratchy seats,
shifting position,
will appear again
in my tunnel vision.

The yellow headlight
whitens
like a miner's lamp,
as the local curves into the crack,

as the mind's eye
searches for reason
in the buried
city of the lost.

Behar-Bechukotai

In the sixth year,
I went out into the fields.
The corn was rising on its roots
like a standing army
of spears.

And the bull rushes
in the Meadows flew
across my vision,
renewed,
a green plain.

A white plastic pipe, curved
at its top, bends
from the black, brackish pool,
like an egret,
eye and mind motionless.

I was born
in 'forty nine,
my life the Jubilee
year extended
into God's.

My hands
are your hands, my line
extends itself in you,
my words
like bubbles in the marsh.

Shoftim

Others spread out their yoga mats
under the sun and moon.
I opened a book.

Find me
in the margins of the page,
the scribbled jottings.

These are the marks I make
on the borders of existence,
the cut edges of the river,

scraps of fabric stained
with the oil of the hills,
the machinery of cities.

Open the olive
to the pit of youth,
heresy at the center.

Who can tell me
the shape of the letters?
Bring me two witnesses

to the *Ketubah*.
I plant my tree
in the desert of the truth.

Ki Tetze

You possessed me
like burned dinner in the house,
smelled at the door.

If we did the unseemly,
unseen, bruised,
who could accuse

different equals,
like the hand
passing over the eyes?

Let me drink
from the spilled dish on the table.
None is more beautiful

than you.
Let the sages debate
who rules.

And the pages turned
like post-its
stuck in the street,

days in amber,
pressed in the asphalt,
tar impregnated sheets,

irreconcilable
white light and yellow.
Eat the yolk.

Ki Tavo

I opened the door
to you, words
for the bird of the air.

The walls were screens,
the slats, a lattice of minutes.
Who read between the lines?

I poured out secrets,
rumble of the rainstick,
flotsam on the tide.

Untie the box
according to the law,
ribbon on the thigh.

You who know me,
hear the turning,
blind side of the moon.

Touch the falling
curl across the cheekbone.
My right arm is in shadow.

Hear me breathing,
leaf left at the window.
Take down the corners of the room.

Genesis

At twilight
at the end of the sixth day,
I opened my mouth,
like a well.

It was late.
The bats flew
by radar, under the rooftops,
demons of the wind.

The world was unfinished,
cracks in the sidewalks
left for me
to repair.

The rain barrel,
filled with wine,
spilled on the pavement,
explosions of mind and air.

Fill the wood
with bodies,
staves linked by binding,
ring of slave and man.

ARGENTINE TANGOS

Freestyles

It could be anyone
with you on the floor,
spinning left and right.

The judge on the dais
balances her stylus
over your balance steps.

The scales of right,
and almost right,
are in the music,

scales re-measured
by your extensions,
free style in air.

Your path is always set
to counter clockwise
for your minute and a half.

Count the measures.
Extend the time
between the rests.

Light falls
from the turning ball,
the ballroom turning in your head.

I fell
from Eden
at the beginning of the set.

I am pulled
back towards Adam,
earth in my mouth,

at midnight.
Night falls.
The stars are little cinders in the west.

Slow Waltz

You placed your hand
just so
on my biceps,
two middle fingertips around the back,
left thumb underneath.

We were hooked
for the long floor,
the pivot turns in the corners,
the spirals like wave shifts
down the plain of the beach.

And the night made
its invisible music,
a sail raised
like white heat
across the face of the bay.

Our foot patterns rose and fell,
the raised dais
was our lighthouse,
the day like a ray of light,
the night like the surface of the sea.

We maneuvered
around the other couples,
handiwork turned to promenade,
our cheeks hot in the arc lights,
our feet arched like the roots of the trees.

Ballroom Tango

We learned the push-pull
of lead and follow,
the sidesteps
of the Cuban walk
along the edges of the night.

Heart tugs
from the bottom of the planet
led us to lifts and dips,
the curve of the mind
in the patterns of the floor.

Roll through
the bottom of your foot,
weight change across the metatarsals,
the spine a stake
perpendicular to earth.

Love curved under
the negative and positive,
the infinitesimal
connection held
in the drumbeat of the instant,

upper registers,
phrasings of the torso,
insistent tango of legs and bodies,
doble cortes
at the core of the world.

Hustle

We danced to forget
a private sorrow,
syncopation of the second beat
before the foot push
back to the center, keeping the shoulders level,

the mind unwound,
spun out like string
towards the wall
mirrored and free,
flexors beveled,

hobby, pastime, obsession,
tear in the minutes' run to nothing,
pull of the body into the basin
of the air, swirl of currents
into the sea.

We dove
from the cliffs of being,
into the vortex, pulled like taffy
stretched from arm to arm,
stretch marks along the tendon.

Lashed to the music,
we heard the sirens,
music of fire trucks
on the avenue,
hooks and ladders into me.

Fandango

I want to be
the fish that swims
into the southern current,
the gulf's fan in the Sargasso,
abanico of abalone and eel.

The light above me
is not my light.
The drift nets reel
in others, krill
abandoned on the spill.

And below, blind mouths
open, close,
tentacles, limitless, phosphorescent,
jellied skeletons,
ghost fish.

Life is smell, feeling,
sound waves on closed ears,
salt spray on a pier,
a hammerhead shark's
dim eyes on sticks.

I am made in this moment.
Vestigial memories allow
me movement, cartilage
bending with the flow,
fan dance of foot and steel.

Continuous Salida

Will I see you in another life,
or will we live this life again,
time travelers, in some foreign future,
like a continuous *salida*
circling round a point?

Would we step differently
varying the path,
forward *ochos* blending
into a dip and bend,
a backwards tango?

The sea rises
on the pier of the day,
lives like posts thrown
into the moon white tide,
summer's ending.

Steps, carry my words
past the pleasure boats,
trawlers on the night ride
beyond the Narrows'
deeper setting.

We are gone with the fishermen.
Who will catch us,
alive in the refrain,
unrestrained love in the netting,
as we breathe and dive?

Diana

Was it the same glance
as in your wedding photograph,
upwards and to the right,
a flash of happiness
under a floppy hat,

that I saw today in you,
your feet up on the kitchen chair,
the miseries of incompletion stilled
in the minutes' silences
under a hunter's moon?

Marriage is a furnace of two minds
in the fixer, acid baths
of wrong and right,
images developed in the lab
outside the lance of understanding.

I hang up the stills
on a clothes pin,
the gray scale in shadow on the strip,
their slotted edges made
for one turn on the wheel.

I beg grace
from the projectionist,
touch ups in flesh and brush,
a face made by the chemicals of time
in all the illusions of the real.

Regatta

Who invented the black brassiere,
the red flesh of the precipice,
the black puck at the hockey mouth,
legs spread around pipes,
defending against the goal?

Offensive is the best defense,
a screen name for the mind
as it travels over body parts,
the horizontal heaven of the night
displayed in white.

We played behind the net,
sea smells in the eyes,
the hands' hovercraft a bone,
swells of wave and thigh,
valley tides.

It was a pause in the fabric of the sky,
a worm hole to nothingness,
a spiral Milky Way of light,
our double galaxy's
black event.

We joined our bodies to our minds
as we piloted the craft
on astroglide, trawling the shoals,
our knowledge of the underside
that makes us whole.

Starfish

I glued the broken
arm of the starfish
back into its body's center,
a white line under
its hundreds of bumps,

around its dried mouth,
its desiccated innards.
Its senses
were now my senses,
feelings of smell and thrust.

What grasp I had
of my subject
was hidden in my fingers,
slow to move
but quick to the touch.

The path I'd taken
across the floor of the shelf
apparently was random.
I'd followed
ripples in the mud.

My mind was pressed
by the weight of the ocean,
all I had ever been,
all that I never was,
one life, one cell.

Queen

Your red lace teddy
was effective at night,
petaled chest,
leatherette cuffs,
mussel opening up.

Deep sleep,
dreaming of church—
the words of the sermon
flew like birds
into the vaulted light.

And the choir sang
invisibly like pipes
behind the iron screen's
pierced melismas,
tattooed notes.

We stepped outside
into the rising sun,
mornings on the lawn,
the hide and seek
of children in the hive.

Let the bees come,
order in hexagonal cells,
life imprisoned
by order of the queen,
the everlasting one.

FERNCLIFFE

Paul Soldner

World kiln,
man the clay,
sun on the salt
made blushlike pinks and reds
on a pot as tall as a room.

So God made Adam.

And the hand of the mind
is ready to receive
the word as carbon.

Seasick on the wheel,
you tied yourself
to the earth's spin,
the mast of the siren,

eternal turning
of the Snowmass aspens
opening their hands
to the mountain wind.

Soldier of raku,
conscience was your object,
the solid moment
seeking nothing,
no solder in the slip's
oxygenless chamber.

Ardis James

The names of the days
are quilted into weeks,
the sun, the moon, and the Roman gods
in the black thread of Valhalla.

You climbed
Delectable Mountains,
traveler in pink, white, and green
with a bag of fabric.

So we are turned
on the Mariner's Compass,
the squares of the years
stitched into pattern.

I am hung
on the wall of the real,
a Maker Unknown's
temporary anchor.

Frank W. Lewis

You returned
five times from the slaughterhouse,

the rising tide
that sank the rising sun,

decryptions
of the Finland Station,

Adam's anagram
mastered by one.

Friedman found you
alone in the vault—

your mind's ranked
stacks of books,

cast iron letters
in weekly blocks.

What was the cryptic
code for God,

the visible world's
invisible name?

Herschel Schacter

I was never free of the camps.
The Little Lager left its stain
on the ceiling, spreading
water and blood.

I stared down from my bunk
on the stacked wooden planks.
His peace was not for me,
God, the ritual slaughterer.

I knew the uniforms
of the ghosts.

A dry sea parted
the living from the dead.
A shochet
cleared the coasts.

I am alive
when you hear me,
Mother and Father, fearful
shadows in the loess.

Alice Kober

I needed an *aide-mémoire* to remember
the letters on the tablets
in their indecipherable crypto-Greek.

I put my days into boxes
card catalogues cut from Lucky Strike cartons,
the ten thousand words of Linear B.

Can I decipher the Aegean,
millennia of phrases that sailed
across the Bronze palaces in ruin?

Who will file me
in sheaves of correspondence,
antiquities of mind and script?

I inscribe my time on clay tablets,
pictograms of chariots and horses.
I let fly the arrow of the world.

Charles Rosen

These are sleeve notes
on the Classical Style.
Let them slip out of your hand
into the abyss,
the black keys that swallow everything
like the inside of a lacquer bowl,
the space around the page,
the dive.

The twelve tones
of the Western scale
cover heartbreak and jokes,
the twenty six letters that make a code,
a moment's poetry derived
from nothing more than air,
more than the names of the composers known
as symbols, Mozarts of the rose.

I began with Haydn, years ago,
the symphonies of heart and mind
believed by people for a time,
then pulled apart by theory,
string quartets explained in prose,
the score always behind me
as I wrote, the search for the unplayable
domination of the notes.

Track

And what of the vast middle,
mid-life, mid-century,
mid-sentence,
days filled with children,
degrees of understanding?

We ran at the center of the track,
around the high jumpers'
pool of sand, inside the circle.
Under us,
crushed cinders.

Clouds like ash
filled the sky,
sky writing
from a distant land,
the world's rotating oval.

A hammer thrower
at the edges of the stands
wheeled,
his hands,
concentric circles,

the curl of the shoulder
furrowing the fields,
the weight of the millstone
following the wheel,
the absolute's fallen torso.

Jacob

Maybe it was
my mother's miscarriages,
and the silence in the house,
the long hall of memory,
my still born sister
and the dead twins,
that made me
a melancholy man.

Daybreak. The sun rises
south of the Freedom Tower,
its spike in the sky of being,
an island of the mind
floating in the river,
under a turning wind,
that carries us
like a mother.

I wake up
in the bright light of heaven,
the fence still
against the side of the house,
no barrier,
and the arch of the great oaks
aligns with my walk,
my shield.

How can I live
in the eternal present,
the ladder of the moment
placed at my footsteps?
An angel is waiting
for me to climb
noon's
wrestling tree.

Crossing

A steamboat sailed from Cuba
around the swamp of the Sargasso,
mid-war, mid-century, mid-ocean,
into a colder sea.

In a green dawn,
my father's first family
slept below deck,
wife, nurse, and children.

Friends of that passage
played cards on anchored tables,
chance shifting
the hands given.

Did I choose
the path I've taken?
The valley of the past
is my hooked mountain.

What I climb
is backwards, driven,
my burden,
my manifest.

Siesta

I slept too much,
napping through revolutions
of mind and eye,
the politics of pleasure.
I left the stadium before the final goal.

Afternoons in bed, I dreamed
of Amazonian rivers,
darts in the underbrush,
mahogany jungles,
dugouts running below the light.

I missed the communal
flicker of the day,
wing tips of talk, monkey chatter,
the red backed tamarins
as they scratched for lice.

Slothful, anti social,
I hung in the understory,
air plant, breathing branch,
orchid in my nest of feathers,
stalk of memory and night.

And the world wheeled,
infinities of cities
above me in the sky,
languages, extinctions of the word,
elliptical fragments of the fire.

Liberty

How much longer will I see the light,
the trees in their infinite wisdom,
the towers of the forbidden city
always across the Hudson,
unreachable spires?

The white sun retreats behind the mists.
The yellow moon presides
over Venus and Jupiter's
rare conjunction,
the bright stars of a dreaming mind.

Where will I see you
after the apocalypse,
in what cave or safe room stocked
with memories of children
shouting, running with the tide?

The river moves towards its labyrinth
under the Verrazano,
the damaged corals of the gulf,
and the drop off the continent
into the clashing, widening trench.

Who will save us
from our Middle Passage,
slaves of the white ship as it passes
the iron lighthouse
with its troubled hand?

Hammerhead

I wake
in the still hour,
turning over the sand.

Grandfather pulled me away
from the hammerhead,
thrashing on the planks.

Date palms waved
over the cabanas,
fluttered like his heart.

In winter,
I walked the silent halls
of the sick man.

Mother whispered.
My nose in her coat,
I held her hand.

No one returns
to the one path
they passed on.

Forest leaves
cover the trail,
sunbreaks in the canopy

like gill slits,
spilled glitter
of time and doom.

Hydrangeas
> *"Such is the recurring cycle"* —Polybius, *"Histories"*, Book VI

What kept me going was the cycle of the world,
the double headed axe of time's
creation and destruction,
endless like the rain,
the halberd of revolution.

So the hydrangeas rose
out of the tended mulch,
in their range of red and blue,
thousands of flowers joined at the stem,
democracy of procreation.

When the light failed,
we cut them.
So the notes from the piano stayed
in the air a moment
under the archway of our room.

Be a book's page,
servant to the letter,
a pencil point,
pinprick in the blind
of the night sky, one light.

Be a seed
blown away
by the interstellar.
Plant yourself
in the comet's ice.

Francis Klein's chapbook *Podebrady* was published by Finishing Line Press in 2011, and his chapbook *Untouched by Morning* was published by Finishing Line Press in 2012. His work has appeared in *Mudfish 18, Fear of Success, A Letter Among Friends, red herring ii, Lion Rampant, Penumbra, Oberon,* and *The Ledge*. He was a finalist for the 2015 and 2016 Richard Snyder Prize of the Ashland Poetry Press and the 2012 Many Voices Project of the New Rivers Press, a semi-finalist for the 2011 Word Works Washington Prize, a semi-finalist for the 2008 Richard Snyder Prize of the Ashland Poetry Press, and a semi-finalist for the Blue Lynx Prize in Poetry in 2012. He was a finalist in 2007 in the Atlanta Review's International Poetry Competition, a semi-finalist for the Paumanok Poetry Award from Farmingdale State College, and also received an award from The Mississippi Valley Poetry Contest. While attending Harvard University, Francis Klein studied poetry with John Frederick Nims and also received the Dante Society of America Prize for an essay on the *Inferno*.

Francis Klein lives in New Jersey with his wife, Diane Niederhoffer Klein, a clinical psychologist, and has two adult children. In addition to his career as a writer, he is a graduate of Yale University School of Architecture. His architectural practice focuses on contemporary and historical work in New York and New Jersey.

www.ingramcontent.com/pod-product-compliance
Lightning Source LLC
LaVergne TN
LVHW041506070426
835507LV00012B/1362